ENLIGHTENISM

21st Century Solutions for Overcoming Pain

Enlightenism

Enlightenism Reviews

Parent from the San Francisco Bay Area
"As a parent, I found that by reading this book on Enlightenism, it helped me to begin communicating more effectively with my children. I became more mindful of my behavior and the words I used to discipline them. It really opened my mind to understand how I was using the same beliefs and values that my parents taught me. Basically, Enlightenism inspired me to search for a new way to express myself as a parent."

Former alcoholic
"After reading Enlightenism, I started to rethink the methods I had used to stop drinking. When I took my first drink, I didn't think about my beliefs and values. All I can say is this book has helped me to overcome my fears of relapsing into alcoholism."

Overcoming pain from failed relationship
"When I began reading the book, I began to change my attitude toward my Ex. I now realized that it wasn't all his fault. I was also personally responsible for bringing him into my life and for my own behavior, which resulted in our divorce. I must tell you: It was very difficult for me to accept any responsibility, because I thought he had done me wrong. That's all I could think of until I read Enlightenism."

Enlightenism

ENLIGHTENISM

21st Century Solutions for Overcoming Pain

MALCOLM KELLY

BYE PUBLISHING

Sacramento, California

For information address:
National BYE Society
BYE Publishing Services
P. O., Box 582016
Elk Grove, CA 95758
916-529-3119

Web site: http://www.nationalbyesociety.org

Library of Congress Control Number: 2018900260
ISBN: 978-09656739-9-0

A SELF-ENLIGHTENMENT BOOK
Printed in the United States of America
First Printing: 2018

DEDICATION

I dedicate this book to those who are unwilling to tolerate pain from their beliefs and values of lack, limitation, and struggle. I also dedicate it to my mother, Arlene Patterson, who first encouraged me to believe that I was smart, and capable of writing a book of this magnitude and sagacity.

Enlightenism

ACKNOWLEDGMENTS

I am grateful to my wife, Carolyn, for suggesting that I write the book. It was her constant prodding and encouraging me to write, even though I didn't see the need to write another book. Thanks Carolyn for being the initial catalyst for my writing this book, and for the helpful comments, questions, and insights you provided throughout the process to completion.

I am thankful to the members of the National BYE Society for providing me with a forum to crystalize my ideas on Enlightenism. Your numerous questions on Enlightenism caused me to search for ways to simplify it so others could also benefit from this breakthrough in consciousness.

Special thanks to Pamela Collier for reading the manuscript and her suggestions and thought-provoking questions that assisted me with clarifying Enlightenism.

I am especially thankful to my son, Tshombe, for reading the manuscript and his insightful, thought-provoking comments on how to simplify Enlightenism for those who are unfamiliar with it.

Enlightenism

CONTENTS

Enlightenism

Introduction

I am writing Enlightenism to share with readers a power-ful new discovery in consciousness. If you have ever asked, "Who am I?" then Enlightenism is a must-read book for you. It answers this question and others sought by those seeking greater power. This is a powerful self-awakening book with a proven Enlightenism formula for you to wake-up yourself and claim the Greater Power of Enlightenism.

Enlightenism is a 21st Century holistic philosophy that describes a power greater than societal definitions of race, color, gender, religion, age, education, and status. When I began my work in consciousness, I wondered if I could ever overcome what others had taught me about power and my worthiness to possess it. This inquisitiveness led me on a journey through the deepest realms of consciousness within me. I felt like so many others who sought solutions to over-come their problems but didn't know where to look.

My first instinct was to do what I had always done and ask someone to tell me what to do. I didn't think of my-self as being powerful or knowledgeable to solve my own problems. It's a powerless feeling to want power and not know where to find it. This is why I am writing Enlightenism, because there's a need for us to know how to solve our own problems.

If you're willing to stop tolerating the pain from societal definitions in your life, then it's important to first understand who created the pain. The book's main thesis is to unravel misinterpretations about who is responsible for the pain and problems in your life. My goal is to first shine light on the distortions preventing you from recognizing that you are the creator of your own pain. I do this by describing the process for creating pain, and then presenting a formula for overcoming it.

When you live in a toxic environment for too long, you learn to accept pain as a natural part of life. Since you live among others affected by varying degrees of pain, there's really no reason to search for solutions within you. So you learn to tolerate pain by accepting yourself as its victim.

Nevertheless, I am describing a way out of pain. It took me fifteen years of research in consciousness to understand how to overcome my pain. Before you get carried away with the statement; just remember I'm not special. I am someone like you who wanted freedom from the seemingly never-ending pain in my life.

I am sharing insights with you from my work that led me to Enlightenism. Enlightenism is the colorless, faceless, and formless unconditioned consciousness within you and me. You may have heard others refer to it as the spirit or greater power.

Regardless of how it's described by others, if you want to know how it works, then you must discover it for yourself. I am defining it as unconditioned consciousness. When you stop accepting yourself based on race, color, gender, age, religion, status, and education, you will discover that you're naturally whole, perfect, and complete. In other words, you're nothing like the person you've been cultivating all your life.

The decision to wake-up from the toxic nightmare where you're being chased by the ghosts of lack, limitation, and struggle is one only you can make. You must decide for yourself to wake-up and choose to travel on the path that leads out of toxicity or continue on the one you've traveled all your life.

When I began to slowly, and with much resistance, wake-up, I couldn't believe how thoroughly I had been misled by others. I initially felt angry for waking-up. I sought ways to defend and rationalize my pain. After a while, I began to understand the deeper meaning of self-discovery. I was no longer unwilling to deny that my beliefs and values are responsible for my pain.

I describe toxicity as an illusion created from the minds of your Guides. Even though it appears as reality, it's still an illusion, but it's the only reality you remember. Your life in toxicity began with your Guides – parents and society – teaching you how to survive in a toxic, unjust world. When you accepted this training, you could no longer accept yourself as whole, perfect, and complete.

Some may believe the pain and victimization I am

describing don't apply to them. I remind you, I had similar denials before and during the writing of the book. And like you, I didn't believe I was victimized by my beliefs and values, nor was I willing to accept myself as a victim. I thought being a victim applied only to those living in the inner-cities. I also believed, incorrectly, they were victims because they lived with high unemployment, unimaginable daily crime, harassment from law enforcement, and so forth. I closed my mind to the truth about my own pain and victimization.

While Enlightenism is not unique to any racial group, some may interpret it to be race-based because of my race. I want to assure all of you that Enlightenism is colorless, faceless, and formless. It is within this consciousness that you can perceive yourself without toxic distortions of race and color. If you're unwilling to free yourself from these distortions, then the Enlightenism formula will not work for you. Similarly, if you are serious about changing your life, then I guarantee the formula will work for you.

The book describes four freedoms as keys of the Enlightenism formula to overcome the lack, limitation, and struggle in your life. I am describing the four freedoms as the clarity to unmask toxicity and expose it as an illusion. They also represent the clarity you need to achieve the Greater Power of Enlightenism. Otherwise, I would be writing a book from the perspective of "Keep Hope Alive" or similar inspirations that keep you struggling for survival in an illusion. In other words, I would be writing about themes and solutions familiar to you.

I am choosing to write about solutions unknown to my

Guides. The book describes these solutions as an awareness-of-being where you acknowledge yourself as the creator and liberator of your pain. This new awareness-of-being is born from within the colorless, faceless, and formless Enlightenism consciousness. It is the consciousness where you're not the victim of toxic beliefs and values.

I describe Enlightenism as the clarity to understand you're greater than your beliefs in lack, limitation, and struggle. I also use the Enlightenism formula to distinguish between toxic desires and enlighten ones.

The Enlightenism formula consists of clarified desires. These are the ones cleansed of toxicity. They exist in your intuitive or unconditioned consciousness as freedom. This means they are free of toxicity and denials about the Greater Power of Enlightenism within you.

When you create a clarified desire, you stop playing games with yourself. You see the folly in searching for freedom in people, places, and things. When you stop playing with yourself, you stop searching for freedom and begin accepting it as something you already possess. I found this distortion to be the most difficult to overcome,

Nevertheless, the Enlightenism formula describes the four freedoms as the clarity to stop playing with yourself. I found the four freedoms helpful during periods of doubt and stubbornness about the value of my work. Even though the work is slow, tedious, and seemingly without a visible end, the four freedoms keep you focused on your goal, not on your pain.

Similarly, Enlightenism, unlike some other traditional

self-help books on spirituality and inner-mind power, describes solutions for overcoming your specific pain. I tried many programs that didn't work, because they didn't present solutions for overcoming the pain from my beliefs and values in societal definitions of race, color, religion, gender, age, education, and status. I was too deeply rooted in these toxic beliefs and values to believe I had the power to overcome them on my own.

It's important to understand that accessibility to Enlightenism requires a cleansed mind. You gain access to this great power by accepting yourself as a creator. This is the awareness-of-being you achieve after you unmask toxicity, and perceive it as an illusion. You cannot enter into Enlightenism with toxic beliefs and values from your former awareness-of-being. Your new awareness-of-being contains its own beliefs and values.

Enlightenism describes the causal connection between your beliefs and values and your awareness-of-being. Your understanding of this causal relationship is essential to your work of creating a new, toxic-free awareness-of-being. Everything flows from your awareness-of-being. It is the cause of pain and the liberation from it.

Similarly, it is your awareness-of-being that determines what you think of yourself and others. You cannot exist without it. This means you must recondition your new awareness-of-being to perceive itself free of the one overwhelmed by lack, limitation, and struggle. For you to become another person, you first must unlearn the beliefs and values others taught you.

This unlearning process doesn't mean forgetting what you have learned, but releasing your attachment to the certainty of the information. In other words, you are unlearning by learning to depend and trust Enlightenism. I describe this "born-again" process as unlearning powerlessness and learning how to use imagination to create a new person. While this unlearning process may appear to be impossible, it is much easier than you think.

Meanwhile, when I first began writing Enlightenism, I envisioned it as a workbook guide to overcome illusions of lack, limitation, and struggle. I wanted others to benefit from my work in Enlightenism to overcome these illusions. The more I wrote, the more I realized I am writing about something more expansive: a powerful breakthrough in the overall freedom of the mind. This is the freedom that has eluded generations of freedom-starved victims.

The book's value is determined by your beliefs and values. It's your awareness-of-being that will determine its benefits to you. Nevertheless, I am confident if you read the book with an inquisitive mind, you will benefit from the insights.

Meanwhile, I remind readers to not use the Enlightenism formula as a crutch. It is a formula that, if used properly, you can achieve the power to overcome your pain.

NOTES

Chapter One
Personal Responsibility

During my lifetime, I have observed thousands of people who have been willing to accept less, rather than work to realize more. These individuals typically believe that it's natural to struggle, live in poverty, and achieve success and wealth by admiring someone else's accomplishments. To them, success and wealth is a far-away dream found in the history of the dead. This type of thinking causes them to tolerate pain, while waiting on someone else to tell them when it's okay to change.

A good illustration of this point is a conversation I had some years ago with a homeless man in Oakland, California. I was on my way to the Post Office when he stepped in front of me and pleaded for some change, which I gave him. I had responded to similar requests before without giving it a second thought; however, this time it was different. I don't know why, but it was.

Even now, after so many years, this conversation is still indelibly etched in my mind as if it happened today.

I begin to stare blankly into his face. I am momentarily

frozen in my thoughts. After several moments of reflection, I suddenly, out of the clear blue say, "Excuse me brother, but how long do you plan to stand out here asking people for money?" And before he can reply, I ask, "Don't you see yourself doing something else?"

"Hey man, I'm tired of this myself," he replies defensively. "I'd like to get a job; buy another house and live large like the rest of you– "

"What do you mean?" I ask.

"Well," he says, pausing for a few moments, "Before living on the streets, I had a nice home. Then I lost my job. Next thing I knew, I started drinking a lot. From there, it was all downhill. And then suddenly, I find myself out here living on the streets."

"Hey, if you did it once, surely you can do it again," I say, offering him encouragement. "You seem to be fairly intelligent. Perhaps if you stopped drinking for a while, get into a rehab program, you probably could get back on your feet."

"Maybe?" he replies. "I don't think I'm ready yet."

"Why not?" I ask.

"Man, you just don't know the half of what's happening out here," he says sarcastically.

"Then help me to understand," I reply.

"Well, for one thing," he says, "I get hassled all the time by the cops. They're always hassling me about my ID, when they know I don't have one."

"Why don't you get one?" I ask.

"Now you tell me what address I'm going to give them," he replies laughingly.

"I see," I say chuckling. "Just out of curiosity, how long have you been living on the streets?"

"Oh, close to four years now," he replies with a disappointed expression. "But it won't be long now."

"Why?" I ask. "What's up?"

"I've got a great idea that's going to put me back on easy street," he replies laughingly. "I'm just waiting on the right person to present it to. Then, just like that, I'll be back on easy street."

"I hope so for your sake," I say skeptically. "I don't think it's quite that easy."

"I feel you," he says. "I know most dudes like me don't ever get off the streets, it's going to be different with me. Watch what I tell you."

"As I said earlier," I reply, "I hope it works out for you."

"I know it will," he replies confidently. "I'm going to beat this homeless thing."

"Are you aware that homelessness is just a state of mind?" I ask. "Your home is determined by what you think of yourself. It's not so much a physical place as it is a conscious one."

"I don't know about that," he says, looking toward the sky.

"I'm making the point," I say, gesturing with my hands, "that what you think of homelessness affects us all. Most of us fear it, because we don't understand it."

"I never thought about it like that," he says, with a befuddled expression. "What you're saying makes sense, but I just don't think I have the confidence to do it right now. Maybe later—"

"Why do it later," I ask, "when you can do it now?"

"Because," he stammers, "I just don't believe I can do it now. I guess you can say I just don't have the determination or confidence in myself to do it now."

"I think at some point soon," I say, "you're going to have to find the will. Don't you agree?"

"I guess so," he replies. "But right now, all I do is daydream about it. It doesn't go any further than that."

"Only if you continue to believe this about yourself," I say, giving him a light pat on his shoulder.

"I guess I'm hoping for a miracle," he chuckles. "Bottom line is: I just don't believe I can do much about my situation— "

"That's too bad," I interrupt.

"It is what it is," he replies.

"Yeah," I say sternly, "but it doesn't have to be. You can

do something about it."

"What?" he replies angrily.

"Take some time to understand yourself," I say, encouraging him to believe in himself. "Try to understand the beliefs and values that caused you to become homeless."

"I don't follow you," he says, looking puzzled. "It's not my fault. I didn't lose my job on purpose. I only started drinking because I was too embarrassed to face my family. So, I begin to hit the bottle a little hard. If anything, you can say I'm a victim of circumstances."

"I'm not going to allow you to play the victim here," I say, looking him in the eyes. "It might seem that way to you, but if you stop and think about it a little deeper."

"What do you mean by thinking about it a little deeper?" he says, looking puzzled by the suggestion.

"Well, if you look a little deeper," I assure him, "you'll see that while your actions seem innocuous or harmless when you make them, their cumulative effects are ultimately responsible for the decisions that led you here."

"I'm not buying that, man," he shouts, removing his cap and scratching his head. "Are you some kind of preacher?"

"No, I'm not. I'm an Enlightenism Speaker and Trainer. I help people to solve their own problems."

"I thought so," he says laughingly. "Most dudes like you talk all that positive, upbeat talk, but I bet you haven't been homeless yourself?"

"Fortunately, I haven't," I reply. "But like you and everyone else, I'm dealing with my own problems."

"Like what?" he says.

"Like accepting personal responsibility for the conditions in my life. Hey, you can't change, unless you first accept responsibility for the things you're trying to change."

I reach into my briefcase and hand him a pamphlet on Enlightenism and say, "Take a look at this pamphlet; it explains my Enlightenism work."

I extend my hand for a handshake and say, "Hey, it's been nice talking with you, but I've got to run to a meeting."

"Nice talking with you too," he says, reaching to shake my hand. "I hope I see you again. By the way, do you think this Enlightenism stuff will help me to get off the streets and back on my feet?"

"Only if you're serious about changing," I assure him. "And if you are, then come to one of our Enlightenism discussions on Wednesdays at 7p.m. down on 14th and Broadway,"

I hand him a flyer with the information and say, "It's free."

"Thanks man," he says, I appreciate it, "If I can, I'll try to make it this Wednesday."

"Okay," I say, turning to leave. "Take care, and I'll look for you on Wednesday."

As I walk away, I wondered if he would even come to the meeting. After all, he's been homeless for quite a while. That's when I realize I had drifted back into toxicity by trying to determine what someone else would do. I quickly change my judgments about him and accept that he will change when he's ready to change.

Nevertheless, several minutes later, I continue to dwell on our conversation. The more I thought about homelessness, the more convinced I became that the awareness of homeless is not only present in him, but in all of us. It exists whenever we affirm its existence in our awareness-of-being.

Since my conversation with him, I continue to think about what could have been done to prevent his homelessness. When we recognize that homelessness and wealth have their roots in lack, limitation, and struggle, we can better understand their causes. Even though we are the creator of homelessness and wealth, we still give them power over us.

Whenever we decide to claim power over our fears and desires, we can see beneath them and accept personal responsibility for whatever conditions or problems in our lives. Similarly, by accepting personal responsibility for our problems, we free ourselves from believing others are responsible for them.

Personal responsibility is not a social slogan, but a state of consciousness. And for you to dwell in this consciousness, you first must embody personal responsibility as a natural part of your awareness-of-being a creator. Since you are the creator of your actions, then you're responsible for the results from these actions. It's important to understand that homelessness, wealth, and whatever other problems in your life come from your actions.

NOTES

NOTES

Chapter Two
Who Are You Aware of Being?

When you decide you have had enough pain, and you can't take anymore, your desires are telling you it's time to wake-up from your nightmare. If you feel this way, you can do something about it. You can ask yourself: Who am I aware of being? The answer to this question opens the mind to perceive other possibilities other than the ones you're using.

The Enlightenism formula for waking-up begins with four basic freedoms for creating and expressing a new awareness-of-being. These four freedoms are:

1. **THE FREEDOM TO CREATE**
    *   Create a vision of a new awareness-of-being that's free of societal definitions.

2. **THE FREEDOM TO EMBODY**
    *   Embody the vision in a present-time conception of a new self.

3. **THE FREEDOM OF ACCEPTANCE**
    *   Accept your inner-mind power as the source that you use to nurture the vision through the necessary time

interval —the time between conception of the new self and your work to express this awareness-of-being in the visible, sense-dependency world.

4. **THE FREEDOM OF DISCIPLINE AND ACTION**
   • Discipline your mind to develop and sustain a daily action plan to overcome the toxic beliefs and values imprisoning you by your race, color, gender, religion, age, education, and status. These societal definitions of who you are, represent the toxicity you encounter after you have created and embodied a new awareness-of-being that doesn't contain any attachments to toxicity.

These four freedoms are discussed in greater detail in later chapters in the book. There's a tendency by many Enlightenism neophytes to distrust the four freedoms. This new approach for creating an awareness-of-being may be difficult for you to believe because it seems so easy to do. Nevertheless, for you to create a more powerful awareness-of-being, you first must be willing to unlearn the toxic beliefs and values causing you to believe in powerlessness, victimization, and oppression.

Unfortunately, change is what causes many people the greatest trepidation. For those trained to believe in toxicity, change represents the unknown, unbelievable, and unproven power.

For most people, change, particularly enlightened and self-empowered change, is considered the enemy of toxicity or the status quo. It forces you to accept responsibility for the conditions in your life and environment. Yet the way to your enlightened consciousness requires a willingness to unlearn toxicity. This means your commitment to Enlightenism must be greater than your commitment to toxicity.

I decided to change only after I had reached a low point in my life; a point where I was emotionally and spiritually bankrupt. Many people who reach this point in their lives turn to spirituality, education, or a change in environment. I felt the same way until something, an unknown, yet familiar idea encouraged me to first take a look at the actions that caused me to have these feelings about myself.

It was clear to me that I didn't like this powerless, victimized feeling, and as a result, I was willing to listen to any idea I believed could assist me with overcoming my pain. I also clearly didn't want to spend my time daydreaming about someone coming to rescue me from my own creations. I may have been confused and emotionally drained about the direction of my life, but I was confident that only I could rescue myself from the conditions I had created in my life.

Whenever you reach a point like this in your life, it feels strange. It's a place where you distrust your thoughts and ideas to be greater than your problems. This is the awareness-of-being where you believe your mind is victimized by illusions of lack, limitation, and struggle. You feel your mind struggling to free itself from the invisible web of illusions imprisoning your mind in toxicity. The more you struggle to free yourself from the illusions, the more you succumb to accepting yourself as powerless. This is the way it feels when you're ready to wake-up and begin your inner-mind journey.

During my initial foray into inner-mind work, I didn't know what it meant to look within for power. Even though I had heard people talk about this all my life, no one had ever told me how to do it, except by prayer or meditation. That's why I had no idea what I would discover when I looked within.

The first time I looked inward, I saw memories of myself existing within the historical context of a victim; a powerless individual with no identity other than the one others taught me. As far back as I went, all I saw were countless experiences of me as a powerless victim. I did not see an image of myself as an all-powerful being; nor did I see an image of a deity or any other being outside the realm of my experiences.

It was only after a few minutes of in-depth concentration that I began to sense a slight, very slight, thought impulse. It was so slight I almost did not notice it. However, I felt a presence within this impulse, which seemed to overpower my thoughts on worry and doubt. Naturally, this got my attention. That's when I tried to still my thoughts and listen more closely to the impulse, hoping for a clear sign or indication of what to do next, but none came.

Contrary to what I have heard about other individuals who claimed they had encounters with these impulses, I did not see a bright light, burning bush, or hear a loud voice commanding me to go forth and free my people. The only thing I was aware of was this slight, but powerful thought impulse, making itself known to me. I did not know it then, but this stranger in my thoughts was intuition; my guide to Enlightenism.

Another strange thing happened shortly after I tried to quiet my thoughts, I suddenly realized that to recondition my mind, I needed to have my body and mind free of any outside influences. This was a spontaneous decision, which did not seem attached to anything at all, particularly my inner-mind search for power.

Similarly, I just felt that the impulse was making me aware that it was uncomfortable being in a consciousness influenced by desires of alcohol. This is when I began the work to cleanse my body and mind of the desires for alcohol and other unhealthy foods.

During my work to cleanse my body and mind, I slowly began to trust the silent, powerful, thought impulses within me. This was the start of creating an unshakeable bond of trust between Enlightenism and myself. I now had the self-confidence in intuitive consciousness to guide me on my Enlightenism journey.

These two decisions would become the easiest and hardest part of my journey on the Enlightenism road. Easiest because they were just words, and hardest because I would have to change my belief system and begin relying on an untested invisible idea from within my intuitive consciousness. I had no idea how to distinguish the difference between an intuitive idea and rational one, much less understand how to use it to achieve Enlightenism.

Nevertheless, I began my work several days later, by reaffirming my commitment to trust something that was alien to me. I admit I didn't feel completely comfortable placing my life on the line based on thought impulses or ideas about a greater power within me. Yet this didn't stop me from going forth with my inner-mind work.

One of the problems I had faced since a teenager, and even now as I began my work, was drinking alcohol. It all began with my friends and me drinking wine. We thought it made us cool, hip, and more adult-like. Wine made us feel high. It released many of our teenage inhibitions. We imagined ourselves free from the fears and doubts imprisoning us in teenage minds.

I felt the past and current memories of my desires for wine pushing everything out of the way as they made their way to the front of my mind. I felt my desires for wine were prodding me, no, insisting that I give them special attention.

I now realize there are many people facing similar problems as they begin their inner-mind work. Many are facing problems with drugs, alcohol, and food addictions. As you read the book, your problems may be with anger, money, relationships, social stereotypes, and so forth. And while all these problems seem disconnected from your inner-mind work, they represent actions and interpretations from your current awareness-of-being.

Regardless of the conditions in your life, they are caused by your beliefs and values. When you can accept this as the sole cause of your pain and suffering, you will have begun your inner-mind work in earnest. This is the clarity you need to know that your desires and actions begin and end with the person you are aware of being. You can now perceive the confusion about your desires for outside things to make you feel better as nothing but your mind expressing dissatisfaction with your current awareness-of-being.

In my situation, I wanted to know why I took that first drink of alcohol, I wanted to know what my thoughts, my beliefs and values were during that moment? I began to chronicle my feelings and insights by writing them in a journal, which would become chapters in my first book on Enlightenism and Empowerment.

Afterwards, I would use my foray into intuitive consciousness as a methodology for examining all my beliefs and values. That's when I realized that each belief and value played a role in influencing me to take my first drink of alcohol. I also realized that because of my beliefs and values, I was already a victim of alcohol before I took my first drink. My beliefs and values had already conditioned my mind to accept anger, poverty, racism, fear, lack, limitation, self-doubts, and struggle as part of my lifestyle, which caused me to seek refuge in alcohol.

It's important to know that when you examine your own life, you will undoubtedly discover that your beliefs and values have already conditioned your mind to crave for things outside of you. You believe you need things to make you feel better about yourself. Nevertheless, whether you're aware or not, the beliefs and values from your parents and society are responsible for your cravings for things.

In my case, I was unwilling to acknowledge this fact about myself. I believed drinking alcohol was a craving for manhood. I believed my manhood would be greatly enhanced by alcohol, because of the fun and joy I had observed when other men drank. Obviously, I was disillusioned about manhood and power.

After I understood and accepted what caused me to take my first drink, I was more confident that I could do something about my problem. This wake-up call motivated me to go deeper into the causation and address not only my desires for alcohol, but also my illusory perspective on manhood.

This awakening was the step, the action, that catapulted me into the visualization and imagination process of Enlightenism. This action was powerful enough to motivate me to continue my inner-mind work of imagining myself as a colorless, faceless, and formless being. I had fortuitously created my first vision of Enlightenism.

During the next several years, I performed a visualization nearly every day. There were days when the illusions of lack, limitation, and struggle overpowered me. These were the times I felt sorry for myself and wanted to return to my old habits. Fortunately, I did not succumb to these desires in the same way I had in the past., I was, however, on a rocky road until I reached a point where I was comfortable envisioning and imagining myself free from my core beliefs and values. That's when I noticed my thoughts slowly free themselves from the web of illusions imprisoning me in toxicity.

During this stage of my inner-mind work, I began to experience a deep sense of humbleness: a humbleness far different from the way I had been taught by others. Initially, it was difficult to accept another interpretation of humbleness, other than the one I had used in toxicity to kneel in prayer or sit in meditation.

For me, the things I now wanted most were greater than wealth, prosperity, a good job, social acceptance, and so forth. Now I believed I was looking inward for something greater, something more powerful than my current aware- ness-of-being powerless to overcome the conditions in my life.

During each subsequent visualization, I continued to ex- perience humbleness in the presence of the Greater Power of Enlightenism within me. At this level of awareness, my humbleness had morphed into loneliness. Now I under- stood that my loneliness came from my beliefs and values dissolving into my new awareness of being whole, perfect, and complete.

In other words, I was letting go of my long-held beliefs and values. This made me feel alone. I was lonely for my toxic companionships. I wanted others in my circle of trust to support me and travel with me on my new journey.

The first several times I tried to visualize something oth- er than my powerlessness, I wanted to stop, and return to familiar surroundings. I didn't like feeling alone, with no one to guide me or affirm my work. This was the turning point in my work.

It was clear to me now that if I wanted to free myself of toxicity, then I must be willing to embrace and accept loneliness as part of the Enlightenism journey. If you are willing to experience this feeling, and remain confident in Enlightenism, you will begin to let go of your dependency on others. When you do, you will discover, as I did, that being alone with yourself is being one with the Greater Power of Enlightenism.

Since my initial visualization, the deeper I go into my consciousness, the lonelier I feel. It's not a loneliness of absence anymore, but one of being alone with my new awareness-of-being.

When you're ready to wake-up and discover the Greater Power of Enlightenism, your purpose in life will be revealed to you. It will be clear to you that you were not created to tolerate pain. You were created with the limitless power to accept yourself as whole, perfect, and complete. This is the answer to the question: Who are you aware of being?

NOTES

NOTES

Chapter Three
Visualization and Imagination

The desire to change your life is the first freedom in the Enlightenism formula. It is this desire that motivates you to begin your work to discover Enlightenism by creating your first visualization. The goal of your visualization is to free yourself from the pain you're unwilling to tolerate.

To achieve this freedom, you must listen to, and trust the silent intuitive ideas within you. When you do this, you can create a boundless flow of new ones and unleash the limitless power of Enlightenism within you. These new ideas contain within them the cleansing power to free your mind from the clutches of toxicity.

One of the primary misinterpretations about how to change your life is believing that it takes too long, and you don't have enough time and power. When the desire is strong enough and the commitment firm, then you always have enough time and power.

To take the first step to change your life, you must first believe you can do it. The belief in yourself confirms that you have the time and power to overcome the conditions in your life. It's important to remember that time is a relative term used to place you in a niche of complacency and mediocrity. Your life is only time-based because of your beliefs and values on permanence and your desire for security.

When you are creating a new person from Enlightenism consciousness, time has no power over you. It doesn't matter how old you are today or what type of condition you are in, you are still alive, which means you can change your awareness-of-being.

During the time between life and death, you will spend your time and energy doing something. Why not spend it unlearning toxicity and discovering the greater power in you?

This means your vision of Enlightenism must be free of time limitations. Your thoughts and actions must be present-moment ones. You are now working in Enlightenism consciousness where you accept yourself as being whole, perfect, and complete. Thoughts of future time are nonexistent. When you live and create in a present moment awareness-of-being, you free yourself of the self-imposed beliefs and values that restrict your creativity.

The desire and commitment to overcome toxicity is a powerful force that you must reckon with if you truly want to change your life. The unknown power producing your desires to change connects you with the Greater Power of Enlightenism. If you continue to search for this power within you, you will find it. And it will not only transform your life, it will lead you to your unconditioned consciousness of Enlightenism: a place where all things are possible.

Unfortunately, too many people believe this consciousness exists outside of them.

Similarly, when you trust yourself, you inevitably trust your ideas. For you to effectively use Enlightenism, you must remain committed and confident that the vision you're creating will be toxic-free. This strong, unshakeable commitment, and equally strong confidence in Enlightenism, are all you need to stop depending on others for your power.

This awakened state of awareness is the mindfulness to ensure that your mind remains vigilant and clear as you enter the uncharted parts of your consciousness that are free of lack, limitation, and struggle. This is the awareness-of-being where you discover you're one with Enlightenism. It's the freedom to accept yourself as whole, perfect, and complete. You are now aware of the clarity and power you possessed before you conditioned your mind with toxic beliefs and values from others.

Meanwhile, to create your first visualization, you must discover and accept yourself as being colorless, formless, and faceless. This is the awareness-of-being that represents your freedom from toxicity, and dependence on others to tell you what to do.

CREATING A TOXIC-FREE VISUALIZATION

1. Sit down in a comfortable seat, somewhere alone, away from other people. I suggest you create a place in your house or apartment for you to meditate and visualize yourself possessing greater power.

2. Take several deep breaths and slowly close your eyes. This will allow you to open a new door that leads into the unconditioned consciousness of Enlightenism, and shut the door to your sense of lack in your life.

3. With your eyes closed, imagine your thoughts as formless, faceless, and colorless sources of creative power.

4. Imagine the problems as weeds in your Enlightenism garden of clarity and power. Identify those weeds that need to be removed immediately. Spell out each problem with your thoughts and write them down on an imaginary piece of paper. See the debts, unemployment, fears, worries, self-doubts, addictions, failures, powerlessness, race, color, gender, age, religion, status, education, and so forth as words on the imaginary piece of paper. In other words, give your problems an identity that comes from you.

5. Next imagine yourself as a colorless, formless, and faceless being with the power to create different realities in your life. Use this power to command your thoughts to become active and alive with the energy to travel effortlessly within the boundless space of your mind.

6. Now, slowly command your thoughts to travel away from the awareness-of-being of lack, limitation, and

struggle into a new time continuum where you are free of all problems.

7. From this new time continuum that includes past, present and future time references, see how your life has evolved from past actions to the present moment.

8. While you are in the present moment, see yourself living with power, freedom, abundance, creation, wisdom, love, and peace.

9. From this awareness-of-being, there are no doubts about your power to express many different realities or awareness-of-beings in your life.

10. Now, for you to tap into your Enlightenism consciousness, you must free your mind of the childhood memories as the beginning of your consciousness. Although your childhood will inevitably provide you with valuable insights into how and when you entered into the toxic mind-conditioning process, they will also prevent you from accepting yourself as being born whole, perfect, and complete. For you to accept yourself in this manner, you must recondition your thoughts to become a colorless, faceless, and formless awareness-of-being existing in the Enlightenism time continuum.

11. After you have completed the work above, which will take you some time to do, you are now able to accept yourself as a colorless, faceless, and formless being. It is from this consciousness that you define your awareness-of-being and purpose in life.

12. Whatever you defined as your purpose is the reason for

the body size, color, gender, mind capacity, communication, and artistic skills, and so forth. This means you possess all the power and clarity you need to be the person you were created to be.

13. With your new Enlightenism awareness-of-being indelibly etched in your consciousness, your vision is complete and you are ready to return your thoughts to your body. As you merge your thoughts with your body, command your body to heal itself of the pain, lethargy, powerlessness, and propensity to succumb to toxic beliefs and values.

14. You need a healthy body and mind to do the work to create an enlightened consciousness. Hold this thought for a few seconds, then slowly merge your thoughts and body into a union of Enlightenism marriage.

15. Open your eyes, slowly, and then take a deep breath and exhale while saying "I am whole, perfect, and complete." "I am greater than the I that I created."

NOTES

NOTES

Chapter Four
Creative Imagination and Embodiment

Now that you have finished the easy part of the Enlightenism formula of creating a vision of Enlightenism, it's time to tackle the hard part: Embodiment and acceptance of this vision in the present moment. Some people consider embodiment and acceptance of a vision as being one in the same. We consider them separately in Enlightenism.

Embodiment is that part of your work where you envision and imagine a clear, toxic-free awareness-of-being and embody its completeness at the moment of conception. Acceptance, however, is when you trust your intuitive consciousness as the power that creates and nurtures your vision of a new person to completion. Acceptance of your vision of Enlightenism is discussed more fully in the next chapter.

You will initially find it difficult to embody a vision of yourself as a new person in the present moment, because of a history of giving greater power to others. Many are accustomed to believing in illusions of powerlessness and victimization as an acceptable lifestyle. It's important to remember that powerlessness and victimization are only temporary relapses in claiming the greater power. However, with continued practice and enhanced self-confidence with your creative powers, you will be able to accept your new awareness-of-being with limited or no doubts at all.

During my travels on the Enlightenism road, I am constantly reminded of the difficulties one has trying to embody a vision of Enlightenism in the present moment. I am frequently asked, "How is it possible for me to embody a vision in the present moment when it's nothing but an idea?" This question is obviously on the minds of all individuals who believe they are powerless to create a new awareness-of-being that's greater than their current one.

I realize that when you are aware of being unemployed, poor, oppressed, victimized, and living in a place where you do not desire to be, it's difficult to conceive and accept yourself greater than your current awareness-of-being victimized by mischaracterizations of yourself. While the current conditions in your life appear as giants to you, they are only reflections from your awareness-of-being a person overcome with powerlessness.

Let's assume you created a vision of yourself as a wealthy person whose purpose is to explain to the world the true meaning of wealth. Let's also assume that when you created this vision you were struggling to make a living. From this awareness-of-being, you would obviously be mesmerized by the realness of poverty in your life.

If someone told you, for example, that you were not poor, unemployed, oppressed, victimized, living in public housing and barely able to eke out a living, it would be difficult to believe and accept yourself as wealthy under these circumstances. Yet, this is what's required of you if you desire to claim the Greater Power of Enlightenism in you.

Several people have asked me, "Why would I feel this way?" My response to this question is consistent: "You would feel this way because your physical surroundings and sensory experiences are confirmation of what you think of yourself."

For you to embody a vision of wealth and success amid this illusion, you first must change your beliefs and values and act as if your new awareness-of-being is already so.

When you clearly see and feel your newly completed awareness-of-being as your natural and organic self, you can then accept Enlightenism as a workable power in you. This makes it easier for you to accept that your vision is whole, perfect, and complete, and all that's required of you is to remove the toxicity blocking its expression.

Another way to perceive embodiment is from the prism of a gifted artist or a creative person. In the case of the artist, he or she first envisions a painting of a person, place, or thing. After the artist accepts the image within as a complete painting, he or she can now begin the work to put it on a blank canvas or paper.

At this stage of the creative process, no one can clearly see the artist's idea or vision of the painting, because it exists only in the mind of the artist. It only becomes visible to others when the artist has completed the work.

Similarly, like the artist, in your work to create a new

person, the process works the same. You first imagine your-self with a toxic-free awareness-of-being. Although you haven't yet expressed the attributes contained within your vision, you have experienced the awareness-of-being a new person. In both cases, the artist and you first envisioned, then accepted, a new idea that was known only to the con-ceivers.

This discovery in consciousness exists only in the deep-est part of your mind where you can perceive yourself from the perspective of being colorless, faceless, and formless.

The more you become comfortable with your mind, the greater power you have to change toxicity into clarity. You are now at the point in the Enlightenism formula where you must make the decision to go to the next level of your in-ner-mind training. Now your motivation for freedom must outweigh your fears of change.

Regardless of how you feel about your work at this point, your desire to free your mind from toxicity means that you're now committed to discovering the Greater Pow-er of Enlightenism. For you to maintain your focus as you persevere through the necessary time-interval between con-ception and expression, you must deny and overcome the existence of your previous self.

Your unwavering trust in Enlightenism is the pow-er you need to free your mind from the illusions defining you by societal labels. This commitment to Enlightenism means you are now accepting your vision as a new aware-ness-of-being.

When you can trust your inner-mind power, you can also

accept that you have the power to create a new vision and express it into the visible world. However, for you to accomplish this great work, you must have a strong, unshakable commitment to your newly created awareness-of-being a toxic-free person. Unfortunately, most people who reach this stage in their work, begin to have doubts about their power. They begin to distrust what they have created, and seek out others for motivation and confidence.

Now is a good time for you to remember that you have the greater power to free your mind from its toxic dependency on others for your beliefs and values. This affirmation of your acceptance of Enlightenism is necessary to sustain you during moments of doubts and distrust. With so much uncertainty and confusion created by others about inner-mind power, it's difficult to believe that this power really exists in you.

When you can accept that your doubts come from the way and manner you conditioned your mind to align with the toxic teachings from others, it's easier to accept you have the power to recondition your mind with new teachings. This means when you believe you're powerless, then you are powerless. You are whatever person that you're aware of being.

It seems strange to accept you are the person that you're aware of being because you believed what others taught you about power and life. Unfortunately, that's what happened to you and others after you abdicated your power to become a slave to toxicity. And until you can free your mind from this web of distortions, you will remain an imprisoned slave in an illusion created by others.

Similarly, at the level of the colorless, formless, and face-less consciousness is where you're able to accept yourself as having been born whole, perfect, and complete. During this stage of your work, you are fully aware that everything begins and ends within your mind. This is the Enlightenism law of cause and effect.

Regardless to what you have been taught by others, you are the cause and effect of the conditions in your life. You are always causing things to happen in your life even when you're unaware of the effects from your causes.

There are times in your life that you believe your actions are not true expressions of the person you believe you are aware of being. During those times, you believe your actions don't represent your intentions. This happens, particularly, during the times when you incur debt, pain from relationships, and regrets from angry outbursts.

During moments of forgetfulness, you forget you're producing effects in your life that are identical in every detail to your awareness-of-being. After a while, and with years of mindless actions, it's easy to forget that your mind-less, seemingly innocuous actions, are representations of what you think of yourself. When you experience unpleasant conditions in your life, you forget you created them, not someone else. These are times when we try to shift the blame to others and unforeseen circumstances.

Nevertheless, when you reach unpleasant conditions in your life, you give them power over you. The more power you give to your creations, the greater the pain you feel. These are your growth moments. The moments when you can change what you think of yourself. Now you're ready to begin your work and accept your vision as a new representation of your awareness-of-being.

Similarly, you will discover the truth about yourself in Enlightenism. It's in this realm of consciousness you can see and recognize the Greater Power of Enlightenism as being you. This is also the part of your journey where you feel vulnerable and may seek solace in your previous beliefs and values. Whenever you feel this way, you must remain mindful, confident, and continue to trust Enlightenism.

Meanwhile, whether you're aware or not of the Greater Power of Enlightenism within you, you must continue to have faith in this indwelling power. This is who you are when you remove the beliefs and values concealing your organic awareness-of-being.

So as the world reels from uncertainty, you must continue inexorably on the path that leads you out of toxicity and into the light of Enlightenism. This is the path where you have the clarity to create a new language, discover a cure for pernicious diseases, and produce other miracles unknown to those in toxicity.

CREATIVE IMAGINATION AND EMBODIMENT ACTIONS

1. Accept your vision of a new awareness-of-being in the present moment and embody it as part of your daily lifestyle.

2. Remove all self-doubts regarding the efficacy of intuition, and eschew the how to.

3. When you face problems in your life, accept them as nothing more than illusions concealing your vision of Enlightenism.

4. Remain committed to your vision, regardless of the time duration between your conception and its expression into the visible world.

5. Trust your toxic-free mind to guide you to the Greater Power of Enlightenism. Embody the greater power as the new awareness-of-being that's free of toxicity.

NOTES

NOTES

Chapter Five
Acceptance and Trust

Up to this point, we have discussed trusting your unconditioned consciousness of Enlightenism. We are now at the point of the third freedom where trust becomes an integral part of your work. For you to express a greater, more powerful awareness-of-being, you must recondition your mind to accept Enlightenism as a new way to think and live. This reconditioning of the mind begins with reaffirming your acceptance of the Greater Power of Enlightenism existing within you.

When you continue to work on cleansing your mind of societal definitions, you will reach the point where you can accept the Greater Power of Enlightenism as being you. Your awareness-of-being one with this power is all you need to know about your work for unlearning societal definitions. This is intuitive confirmation that you are greater than the conditions in your life.

Although there will be times when you're afraid to let go of societal definitions, you will reach the point where they seem to just disappear on their own. When his happens, you're entering the Enlightenism process for unlearning toxicity. The process of unlearning toxicity and accepting Enlightenism catapults you into the energy field where your newly created awareness-of-being is greater than all your possibilities.

Acceptance of Enlightenism is an essential part of your work to express the greater power contained in your vision of a new person. It's also necessary to solidify your trust in Enlightenism, and accept that this great power exists in you. The bond of trust you develop with yourself during this stage is the cornerstone of the mindfulness that you will continue to work on your vision regardless of others' actions.

You will discover the acceptance of yourself as the Creator of a new awareness-of-being that frees your mind of its reference point to toxicity. This trust in the Greater Power of Enlightenism existing within you is your acknowledgment that this is the power used to create and express all awareness-of-beings. Moreover, the acceptance part of the Enlightenism formula is where you lose or detach yourself from toxic societal definitions and dwell within the clarity of Enlightenism.

Some people have found this lost-found relationship has enlightened them to stop their search for power in toxicity. These feelings of loss are merely the reluctance of letting go of beliefs and values you have used all your life. They have become as much a part of your acceptance of toxicity as your name.

Similarly, when you become comfortable accepting the Greater Power of Enlightenism, your feelings of loss will transform into feelings of freedom and clarity. This is the moment you realize you can no longer seek refuge in the dead beliefs and values left behind in toxicity. After you try for a while to go back to your former lifestyle, you will eventually stop trying to resurrect the dead toxic beliefs and values to sit on the throne of power in your mind.

There are times when you instinctively doubt your commitment to continue unmasking toxicity and seeking to become one with Enlightenism. Whenever you feel this way, you will forget who you are by seeking refuge in past memories and giving them greater power than they possess or deserve. You begin to wish for the "good old days," because you're feeling dissatisfied with your current life. Nothing seems to be working the way you want it. You blame yourself for having trusted Enlightenism. This momentary distrust is when you're most vulnerable to try to resurrect dead beliefs and values and restore their powers over you.

Whenever you have these feelings, remember they are in your life because of the doubts you have about the Greater Power of Enlightenism within you. It's also important to remember that when you feel this way about yourself, it's time to reaffirm your commitment to Enlightenism and claim this power as yours. In other words, you must trust, absolutely, yourself as the creator of the new awareness-of-being.

While you're working on your mind to unlearn toxic societal definitions, and relearn how to accept yourself as being whole, perfect, and complete, you stop judging the progress of your work by relying on toxic interpretations of success and failure. When you stop judging yourself, you move closer to Enlightenism and the power you have to guide you through the necessary time-interval where you face the most judgments and criticisms from yourself and others, including those close to you.

The necessary time interval is where you encounter arguments and oppositions to your work to create a new person. Most of the opposition usually comes from parents, spouses, friends, co-workers, and others who, in most instances, want you to succeed. Unfortunately, what they desire is not what you have envisioned for yourself. You are the only one who can know what you have envisioned as a new person. Others will only know after you have completed your work.

Nevertheless, there are some people who stop. Remain mindful of your vision and do not stop, nor try to convince others to support your work. If you become one of these individuals, remember you're trying to free the minds of individuals imprisoned in the toxicity that you're freeing yourself from.

When we create a vision of a new person, we must not only embody it, but have the power and commitment to nurture it through the necessary time interval. Unfortunately, most Enlightenism neophytes fail to recognize that all the illusions present in the time interval are there to challenge their commitment to Enlightenism. The illusions challenge you to let go of long-held toxic beliefs and values and trust the Greater Power of Enlightenism within you.

Similarly, whenever you experience confusion about the value of Enlightenism versus toxicity, you are still trying to hold on to toxicity. The illusions are fighting to maintain power in your life, and since you gave them power over you, they don't want to let go of it. Your illusions can only have power over you as long as you give them power. When you recognize and accept you are their creator, then you stop fighting with yourself for your own power.

It is in the necessary time-interval that you learn to trust your inner-mind power of Enlightenism. You can think of this part of your work as the letting go of one awareness-of-being and claiming a new one. This is where you find the patience, trust, and power to remain firm in your unwavering commitment to pursue your work, regardless of what your senses tell you. At this point in your work, your senses are obstacles. They are obstacles because they rely too heavily on toxicity.

It's important for you to know that while your senses have become obstacles, they are still needed for you to write, speak, eat, and other forms of interpretations. The key is to train them to use the information from your newly created awareness-of-being to do these tasks. This connection of the senses with Enlightenism opens the door of the mind so you know how your senses were created to obey you as their master.

When you forget you are the power directing the senses, you will become confused and find the connection between your vision and the senses too difficult. If this happens to you, then reconnect with your original vision of Enlightenism and reaffirm that you are the creator of the vision.

If you become victimized by what you experience in the time interval, you will continue to depend on others for the emancipation of your mind. If you're accustomed to accepting yourself as poor and powerless, then you will continue relying on government programs, legislation, politicians, and others to solve your problems. If you are employed, well-educated, and believe you have found security in life, you are also accustomed to depending on others to sustain your lifestyle. Unfortunately, in both cases, whether you believe you're poor or wealthy, you are immersing yourself deeper into the illusion of toxicity.

Whenever you distrust yourself, you automatically distrust the Greater Power of Enlightenism. This distrust slows down your work and creates confusion and doubt in your life. Many people believe it's their destiny to live powerless lives. When you have conditioned your mind with toxic beliefs and values, you rely on others to determine your destiny. Your destiny is always determined by your awareness-of-being.

When you completely trust and believe the Greater Power of Enlightenism is within you, then your doubts and confusion about Enlightenism vanish into the nothingness from whence they came.

ACTIONS FOR ACCEPTANCE AND TRUST OF ENLIGHTENISM

1. Accept and understand that all intuitive creations are inextricably tied to the necessary time interval between conception and its expression.

2. Use your commitment to Enlightenism to confront your illusions of lack, limitation, struggle, parents, friends, enemies, lovers, children, leaders, money, physical ailments, and so forth, with confidence.

3. When you encounter the illusions in the time interval, remain committed to your vision of Enlightenism regardless to what is seen, heard, and said by others.

4. Trust Enlightenism with a greater confidence than the information others taught you about an awareness-of-being that defines you according to your race, color, gender, age, religion, education, and status.

NOTES

Chapter Six
Creative Action and Discipline

The fourth freedom in the Enlightenism formula is creative action and discipline. It's important to remember the four freedoms are the beginning actions of cleansing the mind of toxicity. They represent the mindfulness to remain focused on your new awareness-of-being born whole, perfect, and complete. This is the part of your Enlightenism work where you develop a daily action plan to overcome the fears, worries, and self-doubts that accompany most visions as they make their way through the necessary time interval.

Action begins the moment you embody and accept your vision of a new awareness-of-being. This acceptance of your Enlightenism vision of a new person creates a bond of trust between you and your intuitive consciousness. It's also affirmation of accepting yourself as the creator of the new person. The acceptance of yourself as a creator means you no longer believe things come and go magically in your life simply by hoping and wishing.

A major requirement for accepting yourself as a creator is to discipline your mind to focus on the work to create a new awareness-of-being conceived from Enlightenism. It is otherwise impossible to nurture your vision through the necessary time-interval and express it into the visible world. It's only your focused actions on the vision that distinguishes it from a dream or illusion.

We have heard stories of people who have dreams and visions, but lack the power to express them into the visible world. In most situations, their dreams and visions die without having a chance to live. The lack of power comes from their dependency on societal definitions to manifest the visions and dreams. It's also due to their denial of being whole, perfect, and complete. In other words, their visions lack the clarity and power to make it through the necessary time-interval between conception and expression.

When you have done the work to create a clear, toxic-free, vision of a new person, you can command your body and thoughts to work together effortlessly, even when facing overwhelming obstacles. This type of creative action comes from an awakened mind: One conditioned by Enlightenism to overcome societal definitions of race, color, religion, age, gender, education, and status.

There will be times in your work when you may waver in your commitment to Enlightenism. These are the times when your work to free yourself from toxicity may appear as taking blind action. Unfortunately, blind action frightens most of us. It is, however, what you must do if you desire to strengthen your trust in Enlightenism.

Nevertheless, taking blind action and knowing all your actions, large and small, are part of the greater expression of establishing an unbreakable bond of trust with yourself. When you examine your actions in greater detail, you will understand you are unlearning toxicity and establishing a bond of trust with Enlightenism.

Unfortunately, even this awareness doesn't completely remove the doubts from your actions. You still may continue to distrust Enlightenism. During times of intense doubts about your awareness-of-being, you may seek answers in toxicity. This deviation reminds you that it takes time to unlearn toxic beliefs and values.

Many feel this way whenever our actions are inconsistent with our current beliefs and values. After all, we are letting go of years invested in creating a toxic lifestyle. There is always the tendency to keep things in our lives the way they are. We don't let go of our habits easily. This is also the time when many give up on Enlightenism and try to return to toxicity.

Whenever you feel like giving up, think about all the pain and suffering in toxicity you're trying to overcome. And think about all the work and energy you have invested so far to free yourself from your former lifestyle.

Regardless of your doubts, if you really want to change, you must make a commitment to do the work. That's why I focus so much on taking blind action, because it's the beginning of change. It's what you will need to assist you with overcoming your doubts about accepting Enlightenism as your source of power. If your commitment to Enlightenism is strong enough, then nothing can prevent you from becoming the person in your vision.

When you have the desire to envision yourself as being one with Enlightenism, you affirm the person you were before entering into toxicity. This is the awareness-of-being where you are whole, perfect, and complete. When you accept this awareness as your authentic self, your actions are expressed from a position of power, even the loss of a job, house, lover, and so forth.

From the Enlightenism awareness-of-being there is no loss. You're letting-go of powerless interpretations of things that cannot exist in Enlightenism. All your actions in Enlightenism are consistent with your new awareness-of-being. They must, without fail, express that which you, their master, command them to do.

Similarly, I have no doubts that if you're willing to do the work, the Enlightenism formula will provide you with the power to overcome any problem. For it to work successfully in your life, you must accept yourself as a creator rather than a victim. And remain mindful of: "I am greater than the I that I created."

Meanwhile, sometimes it's difficult to interpret your actions as Enlightenism or not. Several years ago, I shared some insights on my Enlightenism work in my book, "Seeds from the Ashes." I think the insights are relevant to your work and actions to create a new person.

"To truly achieve Enlightenism, you must commit yourself to overcoming those beliefs that tie you to victim consciousness. This commitment requires you to look beyond the knowledge of the world and deep within your mind for the road map that will guide you to discover what you really want to accomplish with your life.

"The mind-expansion exercises you have done so far were designed to create a comfort level for you to think beyond your current beliefs. For you or anyone else to change a preconditioned belief, you must be willing to declare its value to your current living conditions. If you believe it works for you, then you will obviously be unwilling to change it. If not, then you are ready to explore some other options.

"To think as a creator, you must acquire the power to think with a free, uncluttered, mind. When you free your mind of clutter and illusions, you are able to create things similar to or greater than the facsimile machine, computer, airplane, television, wireless (cellular) phone, and so forth.

"When you think as a creator, you trust yourself absolutely. This level of trust implodes as confidence within the essence of your mind. The presence of confidence in your actions empower you to go beyond your self-imposed limitations. To possess this type of power, you must believe you can attain it.

"The ultimate power of creativity is that of the Creator (unconditioned consciousness), who created you (conditioned awareness-of-being) and the life forms around you. All great people would give anything to have this type of power. The countless unanswered prayers of victims are attempts to gain favor with this power. What if you could have direct access to such power? What would you ask for if you could talk directly to the Creator (unconditioned consciousness)?

"Well, today is the day you stretch yourself to talk directly to the Creator and understand how the Creator exists within your mind. Yes, within your mind is your intuitive-unconditioned consciousness where all things are possible. For you to access this great power, you first must understand what it is. Second, after you understand it, you must be willing to accept it as being a part of your everyday activities. Third, you must use this power to create a new empowered lifestyle (awareness-of-being).

"Whenever you think of your present living conditions, one thing is absolute: You are what you think of yourself. If you don't like your present lifestyle, you have the power to create many different ones. Today, you are strong enough so you don't have to accept mediocrity as your goal. All that is required of you is to know you have all the power you will need to change your life whenever you choose to do so,

"To develop your mind to express great power, you must first repair the estranged relationship between your illusion-ridden mind and your freethinking mind. Anyone who has become victimized by the illusions feels powerless to think of himself or herself as being greater than the illusions. The illusions of lack, limitation, and struggle are very powerful when they interfere with your actions to change the way you think and live.

"The moment you conquer the illusions in your life, you immediately change the way you act. These new actions reflect a new person. This type of behavior is similar to what some people say is being 'born again.' And in a certain sense, at least consciously, you are birthing a new person into the world. The new person you are creating will no longer think of himself or herself as a victim of unforeseen circumstances. Once you free your mind of the illusions, you will be able to see clearly where you are going.

"When you enlighten your mind to overcome the barriers that prevent you from living a successful life, you will begin to use your mind to create different outcomes in your life. The next step in the Enlightenism process is to reaffirm your willingness to accept that this great power is within your consciousness and you can communicate with it anytime you want to."

TODAY, WORK ON TAKING ENLIGHTENISM ACTIONS

1. Before acting, focus on your vision of Enlightenism and clearly perceive your actions as part of the vision, and you will see Enlightenism.

2. Do you know that your actions are a part of the overall creative process of abundance, success, clarity, and freedom?

3. Become consciously aware of all your actions, even in situations considered to be meaningless or innocuous.

4. Remain confident and act enlightened in the presence of your enemies (illusions and toxicity).

5. Whenever your actions produce intense struggle, self-doubts, and pain; can you stop and refocus on your vision of Enlightenism.

6. Act on all intuitive impulses associated with your vision of Enlightenism, even when they contradict your senses.

7. Trust yourself to take blind action in difficult and seemingly impossible situations.

8. Still your thoughts and know that your actions are not ego-driven or connected to a history of toxic beliefs and values.

9. Awaken your mind to remain confident when facing major problems and act despite the influences from your sensory dependent mind denying the existence of Enlightenism.

10. Remove the urgency of time from your actions and know that you have the time to effortlessly express your vision of Enlightenism.

NOTES

Enlightenism

Chapter Seven
Mindfulness

Many actions seem to happen without a direct connection between the actions and the resulting effects. When you act without having cultivated your mind to function independently of toxicity, you develop unmindful behavioral actions. And without realizing it, these actions result in the pain you're now trying to overcome.

When you decide to take on the challenge of creating a new person, it's important to know that it takes time. The work of creating a new awareness-of-being never ends. You're always aware of being someone.

When you can no longer tolerate the never-ending pain, this is the moment to focus on the mindfulness required to change your beliefs and values. You begin this work by understanding how you frequently act without any clear connection to the person you're aware of being. These actions produce results that appear to have no connection to you. They seem to have magically created themselves to appear as pain in your life.

For you to understand the creator of your actions, you

first must know that the person you're currently aware of being is the creator. The vision you're working to express into the world is inextricably tied to mindfulness. This understanding of causation information is crucial to your work to remain mindful of the beliefs and values you're using to create a toxic-free awareness-of-being.

HOW DOES ENLIGHTENISM BEHAVIOR CREATE A NEW PERSON?

1. When you are able to express forgiveness and love toward those individuals that you believe have caused you pain, you will have made an important step toward achieving authentic Enlightenism.

2. When you are able to envision clearly what you desire to see expressed in your life, you will create the clarity you need to achieve Enlightenism.

3. When you are able to express your new values and moral standards to other people without judgment and expectation, you will have gained the strength you need to trust yourself.

4. When you are able to remove your judgments and opinions about what is right and wrong behavior in others, you will remove these beliefs from your own life.

5. When you take the time to write your moral guidelines on paper, you will enshrine them clearly in your mind and your relationships.

6. When you have compassion for others, you free yourself from judgments about their actions.

7. When you are able to express peace in all your actions, you will have attained peace.

8. When you slip back into toxicity by expressing distrust of others, you must forgive yourself and refocus on the Greater Power of Enlightenism to overcome this behavior.

9. When you can perceive your actions as Enlightenism ones, you will have the mindfulness to use them to change the way you think and live.

10. When you think of someone who is successful and enlightened, you think of the new definition of success and Enlightenism that is being expressed in your new awareness-of-being.

It's important for you to remember that contained within every action is the power that created it. The examination of a problem is the first step in understanding the nature of the problem.

The above Enlightenism insights encourage you to think beyond your current limitations. This will undoubtedly result in improving your mindfulness to act from an Enlightenism awareness-of-being.

Your ability to perceive yourself today as a more enlightened person than you were when you began your work is unfettered clarity. Every change in your activities, no matter how small you might think it is, is a change in the way you think and act. Some changes may appear as innocuous as a single hair on your head, which goes largely unnoticed among the thousands of other hairs on your scalp. Do you fret, worry, and spend a lot of time and energy about losing one hair? Well, you have far more thoughts in your head than hairs on your scalp.

There are many times in your life when you feel that one single incident is a life-changing experience. How many times have you said or heard someone else say, "Man, I wish I had a made a different decision." "If I hadn't become pregnant as a teenager, I could have done so much more with my life." "If I hadn't hung around with the wrong kids, I wouldn't have made some of the decisions I made as a kid."

You can add to the list so many other decisions and actions that have brought you to this place in your life. But no matter how many times you bemoan your past decisions or judge them to have been life-changing experiences, you are still left with the current decision of changing your behavior. The key word here is *current*.

WHAT DO YOU THINK OF YOURSELF IN THIS MOMENT?

After envisioning and embodying a new aware-ness-of-being, and reading this book, and whatever else you have been doing to improve your life, do you think you are presently a very powerful Enlightenism being? What are the attributes you desire to express in your life? Are these attributes consistent with your vision of Enlightenism?

1. Do you feel you are better equipped today to solve your problems than you were several months ago?

2. Are you using the Enlightenism formula to change your awareness-of-being and create the clarity you need to express this in your actions?

3. List a significant problem you have overcome since you began your work to create a new awareness-of-being.

4. List five attributes you believe an Enlightenism person should possess.

5. Do you currently possess these five attributes? If not, why?

6. Do you believe you have chosen the best career or life-style to express your greatness?

7. List five things you believe are expression of Enlight-enism in the work that you're currently doing.

8. Do you desire to change the work you're doing and cre-ate a completely new lifestyle?

9. Do you believe a new lifestyle will give you greater power than you currently possess?

10. When you awoke today, did you feel like a million-dollar lottery winner and you were living the life you always dreamed about? If so, describe this feeling. If not, describe how you felt when you awoke today.

The Enlightenism insights in the book are to assist you with evaluating your current understanding of what you think of yourself, and the value of devoting your life to creating a new awareness-of-being. The work you are doing on your mind must be real and valuable to you. If you don't believe in yourself and your work, then you will abandon it after a short period, and seek the way of least involvement with yourself.

Regardless of what others say or think about you, you must be committed to changing the way you think and act. It will probably take your spouse, friends, relatives, co-workers, and family members some time to recognize the changes you are making in your life.

Nevertheless, you must remain firm in your resolve to trust Enlightenism to guide you in making clear decisions. And, as sure as day follows night, your new actions will produce a new person in the world. This new person will personify your new awareness-of-being whole, perfect, and complete.

To affirm your mindfulness to Enlightenism, practice saying this mantra daily:

"I am greater than the I that I created."

I am mindful of my responsibility to act from the awareness-of-being a creator. I am an active participant, not an observer, in all of my actions.

My work is of value to me and to those who benefit from my insights and actions.

Mindfulness is a state of awareness where I dwell within Enlightenism and accept that I am whole, perfect, and complete.

"I am greater than the I that I created."

ENLIGHTENISM PROCESS

1. CONCEPTION (the idea or vision) is GREATER THAN ITS EXPRESSION (what you have created).

2. FOUR FREEDOMS OF ENLIGHTENISM

   1. My VISUALIZATION AND IMAGINATION is the essence of my perception.

   2. When my CREATIVE IMAGINATION AND EMBODIMENT come together, I manifest a decision of freedom.

   3. Through ACCEPTANCE AND TRUST, I move beyond awareness into the

   4. CREATIVE ACTION that completes work on my freedom.

CAUSE AND EFFECT

PAST of	PRESENT AWARENESS	FUTURE OF
I should have…	I am…	I will be…
I wish I had…	I am…	I hope to…
If I hadn't done…	I am…	I will be...
VICTIM	**EXTERNAL ISSUES**	**NEW PERSON**
POWERLESS	STATUS/RACE/GENDER	ENLIGHTENISM
LACK	RESOURCES, MONEY	ENLIGHTENISM
LIMITATION	UNABLE TO ACHIEVE	ENLIGHTENISM
STRUGGLE	OVERWHELMED BY PROBLEMS	ENLIGHTENISM
DOUBT	DISTRUST IN YOURSELF	ENLIGHTENISM

NOTES

Chapter Eight
The Enlightenism Formula

The work you have done up to this point can be summarized in two categories: First, understanding the origins of toxicity in your life, and second, accepting that you have the power to overcome toxicity and create a new awareness-of-being.

During this stage of your work, it's easy to forget there are still vestiges of toxicity within you. When you become too proud of your work, it's easy to forget there's still more work to do. That's why this summary of the Enlightenism Formula comes after the work on creating and expressing your Enlightenism vision. It's here to remind you not to get too carried away with feeding your ego.

Similarly, it's easy to forget that you are greater than your results. Some Enlightenism neophytes desire to gloat in the results and seek praise from others. When you feel this way, you are relapsing into your previous toxic lifestyle.

Whenever you feel you're relapsing into toxicity, it's time to reaffirm your acceptance of Enlightenism as the Greater Power. I am sharing a proven Enlightenism formula with you to remind you that the work you have done on overcoming toxicity is working. I am also sharing the formula to mitigate any doubts you have about the efficacy of Enlightenism to free you from toxicity.

The formula reaffirms that the Greater Power of Enlightenism is achieved by using a process similar to the one used to condition your mind to believe you're powerless. The work you're currently doing is leading you out of toxicity. And as you feel yourself leaving all that you have known, there are times when you miss your toxic lifestyle.

Nevertheless, unlike your former toxic lifestyle, Enlightenism exists outside of toxicity. It exists within you as whole, perfect, and complete unconditioned consciousness. And unlike toxicity, this awareness-of-being is free from beliefs of lack, limitation, and struggle. When you perceive yourself and others from the prism of Enlightenism, you're not inhibited by toxic distortions.

With Enlightenism you have the clarity to perceive people, places, and things beyond the illusory interpretations others taught you. Unfortunately, when you distrust Enlightenism, the illusions regain their power over you, and you return to your toxic interpretations.

Meanwhile, at this stage of your work, you have attained sufficient clarity to perceive toxicity as something you have the power to overcome. You no longer perceive toxicity as an obstacle preventing you from creating a new awareness-of-being. You have done the work to understand the formula, and use it to achieve greater power and clarity.

ENLIGHTENISM FORMULA FOR CREATING A NEW AWARENESS-OF-BEING

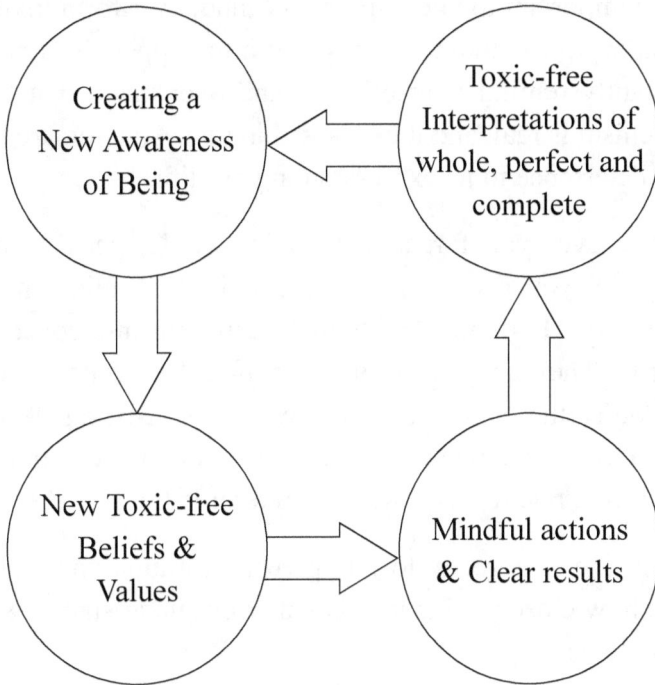

- Toxic-free Beliefs and Values (Refer to Four Freedoms)
- Mindful Actions
- Clear Results
- Toxic-free Interpretations and Judgments
- Redefined Desires for Pleasure
- New Awareness-of-Being

The above formula represents the process for creating an Enlightenism awareness-of-being. It illustrates the development stages you undergo to free yourself from toxicity. This formula is proven to work for those who have the desire and willingness to overcome toxicity and accept the Greater Power of Enlightenism.

It's important to know that you cannot transform toxicity into power without first desiring it to happen. You must constantly remind yourself over and over again that Enlightenism is real, and it exists within you. And you are the only deterrence to its expression in your life.

Whenever you forget that you're whole, perfect, and complete, you also doubt the existence of Enlightenism within you. It's your doubts that keep you imprisoned in toxicity. They come forth in your life whenever you forget you're the creator of your awareness-of-being. When this happens, you must constantly self-motivate to continue your work, regardless of sensory interpretations.

You are now ready to interpret the formula and determine how closely aligned it is with your understanding of Enlightenism.

AWARENESS-OF-BEING

The first and last ingredient of the formula is to live and embody your awareness-of-being. The sole purpose of your Enlightenism work is to create a new awareness-of-being. This new awareness-of-being must be as toxic-free as possible. You now have the clarity to understand that your awareness-of-being determines not only what you think of yourself, but your actions.

When you reach this part of your work, you have assured yourself that the Greater Power of Enlightenism exists within you. You are guided by burning, unrelenting, desires to continue unimpeded on your journey to Enlightenism. You are armed with a new awareness-of-being that knows the way to itself.

The qualities you need to create a new awareness-of-being are ones contained in your Enlightenism vision. When you began your work to create a vision of a new person, you were also creating the attributes or beliefs and values for the person. In other words, you were letting go of toxic beliefs and values and assuming ownership of the ones from Enlightenism.

Your awareness-of-being must originate from within a consciousness where you accept yourself as being whole, perfect, and complete. This is the consciousness that's free of lack, limitation, and struggle. That's why it's important for you to spend the initial time and energy to unlearn toxicity and learn how to embody a new way to think of yourself. Otherwise, your new awareness-of-being will not contain toxic-free beliefs and values of yourself as colorless, faceless, and formless. These are the essential qualities you need to create your new awareness-of-being.

When you work from this level of consciousness, there are few, if any, doubts about yourself as the creator of the new person. Similarly, everything contained within your completed Enlightenism vision is now contained within your new awareness-of-being. When you know this absolutely, you will accept yourself as the creator of your new awareness-of-being.

BELIEFS AND VALUES

The second ingredient of the formula begins with your work to understand and free yourself from societal definitions responsible for lack, limitation, and struggle. This work removes whatever lingering doubts you may have about denying your beliefs and values came from others (parents, teachers, and society). Your parents and society introduced you to the societal definitions of race, color, gender, religion, age, status and education.

Similarly, you also must understand and accept that all actions begin and end within your awareness-of-being. This confirms to you that your current awareness-of-being cannot exist without beliefs and values. Your first priority in creating a new awareness-of-being is unlearning toxic beliefs and values by replacing them with toxic-free ones: The ones used to create your vision of Enlightenism.

Regardless to what others taught you about who you are, you used this information to create your current awareness-of-being. And for the formula to work successful, you must unlearn what they taught you, and create a new awareness-of-being by using cleansed beliefs and values.

ACTIONS

The third ingredient of the formula highlights your non-toxic creative powers. This part of your work is difficult to understand, because in many instances your actions seem instinctive. It's easy to forget that even well thought-out actions come from your current awareness-of-being. You now are required to accept all your actions, regardless of the results, as coming from your new awareness-of-being. And if you're not mindful, you will sometime forget you are the one taking the actions. It may seem circumstances are making the actions for you.

Nevertheless, the acceptance of the results from your actions further confirm and solidify you as their creator. You are now cognizant of the awareness-of-being responsible for the actions. It's important to remember and affirm that the beliefs and values used to create your awareness-of-being are now expressed in all your actions.

You also know and affirm your previous tendencies to blame others for your actions are gone. You are now living in a consciousness that's not guided by lack, limitation, and struggle. The more you trust your new awareness-of-being, the less likely you are to become victimized by your former lifestyle. This deep trust will produce an unshakeable commitment to mindfulness and discipline. After a while, mindfulness and discipline will become as natural to you as the instinctive toxic reactions you're letting go. You will then know the causal relationship between your actions and their results.

RESULTS

The fourth ingredient of the formula is when you fully accept your awareness-of-being as whole, perfect, and complete. This is the clarity required to stop believing you're victimized by the results from your actions. You now possess the awareness to know that all your actions express the desired effects from their creator. In other words, your actions cannot contain within them desires other than yours.

The more you trust Enlightenism as your awareness-of-being, the less time you spend judging the results from your actions as good or bad. When you work in Enlightenism consciousness, there are no surprises from your actions because the results have already been determined by you.

When you accept responsibility for creating your actions, you know the results cannot be greater than you. Regardless of what you interpret them to be, they can never be greater than you. When you forget your role as the creator of your actions, then you interpret the results from this awareness-of-being.

INTERPRETATIONS AND JUDGMENTS

The fifth ingredient of the formula is when you interpret the results from your actions and judge them good and bad, happy and sad, success and failure, and so on. These are the times when you relapse into toxicity and search for toxic interpretations to judge your work. During these moments of distrust, you must remind yourself that you are the creator and interpreter of the results.

It's always beneficial to remind yourself daily that your awareness-of-being determines the power and clarity contained in the results from your actions. This affirms to you that whatever actions you create from an Enlightenism awareness-of-being cannot produce results alien to their creator. So it's fruitless to try and interpret them from a toxic awareness-of-being.

Whenever the judgment tendencies return, you will know you have relapsed into toxicity. When this happens, take your attention away from the judgments and return it to the Greater Power of Enlightenism.

PLEASURE

The sixth and final ingredient in the formula is how to overcome your desires for pleasurable results, Pleasure is one of the most difficult desires to let go. While its roots are in toxicity, it affects your work in Enlightenism. It's been a part of your life since you first desired sustenance from your mother.

The Enlightenism formula is created to change your relationship with desires for pleasure. The previous five ingredients of the formula prepared you to overcome desires for toxic pleasures. They also reminded you that when you work in Enlightenism, you don't immediately let go of your toxic habits.

In other words, when you initially let go, it's not considered a pleasurable experience. You also may feel Enlightenism isn't working properly. It may seem it's causing more pain than pleasure in your life.

Whenever you feel this way, it's important to know that actions from your new awareness-of-being are free of lack, limitation, and struggle. You're freeing yourself from toxic distortions of seeking pleasure in people, places, and things.

During times of great doubts and inner turmoil, you will likely desire to play the victim game of blaming others for your problems. Whenever you feel this way, don't abdicate your power to lack, limitation, and struggle. You must affirm that your new awareness-of-being provides the clarity to redefine your insatiable desires for pleasure. This doesn't mean you eschew pleasure, it means you're not interpreting it from a toxic awareness-of-being.

Meanwhile, the above formula, if used properly, is guaranteed to create a new awareness-of-being. This guarantee is based on your commitment to drop one awareness-of-being and accept a new one. When you do, you will awake from the darkness of toxicity and into the light of Enlightenism.

NOTES

NOTES

Chapter Nine
Enlightenism Health Insights

Enlightenism is a holistic philosophy for achieving the Greater Power of Enlightenism within you. This means it focuses on mind and body. Your body must be in good health to provide you with the energy to do the arduous work required to create a new awareness-of-being.

I strongly recommend you include daily physical exercises to create a harmonious relationship with the creative work you're doing to enlighten your mind. This work also includes creating a healthy diet. And while I suggest you adhere to a vegan diet, which excludes all animal food stuffs, I recognize the challenges this change might present to some. For those who are comfortable eating animal foodstuffs, I suggest you gradually decrease your intake of animal products.

For you to successfully change your diet, you must be willing to let go of eating traditional foods, particular ones that are culturally-based or those that represent affluence or upward mobility. It's important to know that most, if not all, diseases come from the foods you eat and your power and clarity to overcome stressful situations. You have the power to control what you eat and think. This gives you power to choose what foods to eat and what beliefs and values to embody.

During my work in Enlightenism, I have changed my beliefs and values many times. Most of my resistance was towards my diet or my unwillingness to stop eating certain foods, because I liked them. I frequently associated certain foods with my beliefs of success. This association nearly always include memories of my wife and me eating in an upscale restaurant that made us feel good. These memories and associations made it difficult for me to change. I imagine you have similar ones you're holding on to.

There are times in your Enlightenism work when you just feel compelled to resist change. You feel the need to hold on to some things you value, which include certain foods. It is during these times that you are most reluctant to change your diet.

When we are resistant to change, regardless of how small, we affirm our willingness to stay where we are in toxicity. This contradicts the work you're doing to free yourself from toxic societal definitions.

Nevertheless, you have faced many challenges in the work you have already done. This is why I am sharing health information, not as a challenge, but to assist you with transitioning from a meat-based diet to a plant-based one. I am also sharing the information to remind you of how your dietary habits are connected to the work you're doing to transition from toxicity to Enlightenism.

SUGGESTIONS FOR TRANSITIONING TO A PLANT-BASED LIFESTYLE

MORNING

(Begin your day around 6am, if possible)

1. Visualization --- Reaffirm your commitment to creating a new Awareness-of- Being.

2. Apple Cider Vinegar --- Alkaline Treatment before eating

   - 1 Tablespoon of Apple Cider Vinegar

   - 1 Cup, or less, of Non-Tap Water

3. Organic Coconut Oil Gum Treatment

   - 1 Tablespoon of Organic Coconut Oil

   - Swish around mouth for 20 minutes. Work up to this time. At first try 10 minutes

4. Breakfast Options

   - Green Smoothie Suggested Ingredients

     1. Organic Spinach

     2. Organic Almond Milk Drink

     3. Banana (Organic)

     4. Green Plant Juice (Organic)

     5. Avocado (Organic)

     6. Organic Peanut Butter

   - Steel Cut Oaks (Quick Cook)

   - Blueberry Smoothie

5. Physical Exercise (30-45 minutes) Includes Cardio and Weights for Muscle tone and Balance).

LUNCH

1. Spinach Salad, w/Avocados, Nuts, Onions, Tomatoes, Cucumbers, Etc. (No Meat or Fish)

2. Soup – Bean, Lentil, Vegetable, Etc.

3. Vegetable Patty (Soy free & GMO free)

4. Fresh Fruit – Apple, Peach, Nectarine, Banana, and so forth.

5. Green Tea, Ginger, Burdock Tea, etc.,

6. Organic Peanut Butter and Organic Honey Sandwich

7. Snack (Organic Products only)

> Fruits
>
> Raw Nuts
>
> Avocados
>
> Olives

DINNER

1. Combination of the following foods

   - Spinach Salad (See Ingredients from Lunch)

   - Kale, Cabbage, Okra, Squash, Broccoli, Organic Corn (Non-GMO), Etc.

   - Assorted Beans and Peas: Blackeye Peas, Pinto Beans, Split Peas, Lentil,

   - Dessert: Organic Fruits – Apple, Orange, Banana, Blueberry, Peach, Tangerine,

   - Veggie Patty (Non-GMO and Soy Free)

   - Organic Sweet Potatoes, Yams, Irish Potatoes, Etc.

   - Any Herbal Organic Tea

   - Don't eat after 7PM, If hungry, drink water or snack on Apple.

2. Seasonings

   - Salt less Organic Seasoning Mix

   - Turmeric

   - Himalayan Pink Salt

   - Pepper

   - Sun Dried Paprika

   - Cilantro

   - Onions (Sweet Organic)

   - Fresh Garlic

NOTES

Chapter Ten
Enlightenism Affirmations and Principles

ENLIGHTENISM AFFIRMATIONS

SUNDAY

I am greater than the I that I created.

I affirm in this day that I awakened with the knowledge that I am whole, perfect, and complete. I have the Greater Power of Enlightenism within me. This power is all I need to overcome what others taught me about who I am.

Regardless of what I encounter in this day, I remain resolute that nothing changes my awareness of having the Greater Power of Enlightenism within me. Every event and situation are merely interpretations from my aware-ness-of-being. And as long as I am aware of being the Greater Power, I shall perceive myself greater than the conditions in my life.

I command myself in this day to work only on expressing the Greater Power of Enlightenism in all of my actions. I affirm that the Greater Power of Enlightenism is my awareness-of-being whole, perfect, and complete.

I affirm that before I enter into a temporal state of sleep that my thoughts will be fully focused on the Greater Power of Enlightenism within me.

I end my day by accepting that I am the Greater Power.

MONDAY

I affirm today that I am greater than the I that I created.

I enter into this day awakened to the Greater Power of Enlightenism existing within me. I am a fearless warrior without doubt, anger, fear, and worry. I am freed of lack, limitation, and struggle.

There are no problems greater than my awareness-of-being whole, perfect, and complete. I command all the illusions to disappear into the nothingness from whence they came.

I am committed in this day to not accepting the pain and suffering from anyone I interact with as my own. I share my light of Enlightenism with all beings and encourage them to seek the Greater Power of Enlightenism to give them succor.

I affirm that before I enter into a temporal state of sleep that my thoughts will be fully focused on the Greater Power of Enlightenism within me.

I end my day by accepting that I am the Greater Power.

TUESDAY

I am greater than the I that I created.

I awaken this day to affirm my commitment to the Greater Power of Enlightenism. I acknowledge I have no enemies to my affirmation of being whole, perfect, and complete.

I understand and accept that my work is never finished until I have removed all of the toxicity from my consciousness. I acknowledge I am a creator. I am free of all struggles in my life. I am colorless, faceless, and formless. This is the awareness-of-being that guides me in this day.

I affirm in this day that regardless to what I hear and see, I will remain true and committed to doing the work to express the Greater Power of Enlightenism in my life.

I affirm that before I enter into a temporal state of sleep that my thoughts will be fully focused on the Greater Power of Enlightenism within me.

I end my day by accepting that I am the Greater Power.

WEDNESDAY

I am greater than the I that I created.

I begin my day by affirming that I am alive. My purpose in this day is to continue my work to express the Greater Power of Enlightenism in my life. I am a powerful, unstoppable force with no limitations or boundaries to expressing the Greater Power of Enlightenism in my life.

I am on the Enlightenism path because it's the path I have chosen to travel. I affirm my commitment to travel on this path by the work I am doing to express the Greater Power of Enlightenism in my life.

I acknowledge that today is the continuation of my work from yesterday. I accept that every day is one that I am committed to expressing the Greater Power of Enlightenism in my life. Enlightenism is all the food I need to sustain me through the day.

I affirm that I will work to cleanse my consciousness of toxicity throughout this day and when I end my day with sleep, I accept that I did the work to express the Greater Power of Enlightenism in all of my actions.

I affirm that before I enter into a temporal state of sleep that my thoughts will be fully focused on the Greater Power of Enlightenism within me.

I end my day by accepting that I am the Greater Power.

THURSDAY

I am greater than the I that I created.

I affirm I am committed to doing the work to express the Greater Power of Enlightenism in all of my actions. I acknowledge that I am whole, perfect, and complete existing in a colorless, faceless, and formless awareness-of-being.

I acknowledge that this is the day I devote to sitting in solitude with myself. I choose in this day to practice silence, and refrain from talking.

I affirm that whatever thoughts come forth urging me to leave my solitude, I shall remain one within the stillness of the Greater Power of Enlightenism.

I affirm that before I enter into a temporal state of sleep that my thoughts will be fully focused on the Greater Power of Enlightenism within me.

I end my day by accepting that I am the Greater Power.

FRIDAY

I am greater than the I that I created.

I affirm today that I am the creator of everything in my life. I am greater than my results.

I affirm that I am aware of myself as being whole, perfect, and complete. I am committed to removing everything causing me to doubt this awareness-of-being.

I acknowledge I am greater than the conditions in my life. I am enlightened with the clarity of the Greater Power of Enlightenism to see clearly without toxic distortions of lack, limitation, and struggle. I accept that my awareness-of-being was created by me from a colorless, faceless, and formless consciousness.

I affirm that before I enter into a temporal state of sleep that my thoughts will be fully focused on the Greater Power of Enlightenism within me.

I end my day accepting that I am the Greater Power.

SATURDAY

I am greater than the I that I created.

I affirm that I awakened today to an awareness-of-being whole, perfect and complete. I acknowledge I am the creator of this awareness-of-being.

I acknowledge I am committed to expressing in this day the Greater Power of Enlightenism in my life. I affirm that no one can stop me from expressing this power.

I affirm that my thoughts will be focused completely on accepting my awareness-of-being whole, perfect, and complete. I accept myself as the creator of everything in my life. I acknowledge I have the power to change everything in my life.

I affirm that before I enter into a temporal state of sleep that my thoughts will be fully focused on the Greater Power of Enlightenism within me.

I end my day by accepting that I am the Greater Power.

NOTES

TEN PRINCIPLES OF ENLIGHTENISM

1. I acknowledge that I am responsible for the current conditions in my life.

2. I acknowledge that my beliefs and values created the conditions in my life.

3. I acknowledge that I have the power to change my beliefs and values.

4. I acknowledge that for me to change my beliefs and values, I must first be willing to enter into self-discovery.

5. I acknowledge that self-discovery is the gateway to my unconditioned awareness-of-being.

6. I acknowledge that I have the power to express peace, love, and compassion to others and to myself.

7. I acknowledge that I have the power to live my life free of toxic beliefs and values.

8. I acknowledge my responsibility for engaging in mindful parenting relationships with my family.

9. I acknowledge that I have the power to live my life free from all forms of addictions.

10. I acknowledge that I have the power to express happiness and mindfulness in all my actions.

NOTES

NOTES

GLOSSARY

Awareness-of-being The self or person that you accept as being you.

Complete Consciousness free of lack, limitation, struggle, and toxicity.

Embodiment That part of the Enlightenism process where one is able to form a clear concept of the vision of Enlightenism and embody its attributes at the moment of conception.

Enlightenism A state of unconditioned consciousness (awareness-of-being) that produces a clear image of one existing as a timeless, colorless, formless, and faceless being who is empowered to create an infinite number of life expressions.

Greater Power Unconditioned Consciousness A greater power within you that transcends all awareness-of-beings. One's awareness-of-being whole, perfect, and complete.

Illusions Toxic beliefs and values from others that one uses to interpret himself or herself and one's relationship with the external world. A man-made-world created for one to accept as reality.

Intuition Toxic-free inner-mind power. Consciousness that is greater than the beliefs and values created by the senses. One's power to connect with the unconditioned consciousness of Enlightenism.

Organic Authentic awareness-of-being whole, perfect, and complete. To accept yourself existing in consciousness as colorless, faceless, and formless.

Others   Parents, Society, and acceptance of their beliefs and values for your awareness-of-being.

Perfect   Created from the perfection contained within your unconditioned consciousness.

Powerless   Creation of one's awareness-of-being from toxic beliefs and values. Acceptance of lack, limitation, and struggle as a way of life.

Toxicity   Beliefs and values that have a deleterious effect on one's power to distinguish between an illusion and the Greater Power of Enlightenism.

Victim   One who perceives himself or herself powerless to overcome the conditions in one's life without depending on others for guidance. One who relies on the teachings and beliefs and values of others to define one's purpose for living.

Visualization   One's ability to create an awareness-of-being from a colorless, faceless, and formless perspective. Creation from intuitive consciousness.

Whole   The awareness-of-being one with your unconditioned consciousness.

This book was published by BYE Publishing, the publishing company of the National BYE Society, a non-profit 501c(3) organization headquartered in the Sacramento, California area. The vision of the organization is to create an enlightened society that is free of confusion and suffering. The BYE Society's holistic philosophy of Enlightenism is to teach and promote Enlightenism to as many people that are willing to experience this Greater Power.

You can support our Enlightenism work by visiting the National BYE Society web site and making a tax-deductible donation. You can also contact us for information on how to become an Enlightenism Practitioner.

We suggest readers create Study Groups to discuss Enlightenism and share the book with those who share their pain with you.

Contact: http://www.nationalbyesociety.org

NOTES

ABOUT THE AUTHOR

Malcolm Kelly is the founder and president of the National BYE Society. He devotes his time to promoting and teaching the freedom principles of Enlightenism. His work in Enlightenism is a major breakthrough in consciousness for those victimized by beliefs of lack, limitation, and struggle. Brother Malcolm has authored three books on Powers of Mind and Enlightenism. He currently hosts a daily radio show "The Powers of Mind Hour," and writes a weekly blog on "Enlightenism Insights."

Malcolm has B.A. (magna cum laude) and M.A. degrees in Philosophy. He was a student of renowned Philosophy professors, Drs. John Goheen and William Warren Bartley III.

Books by Malcolm Kelly:

The New African American Man

Let There be Life

Seeds from the Ashes

NOTES

www.ingramcontent.com/pod-product-compliance
Lightning Source LLC
LaVergne TN
LVHW021518080426
835509LV00018B/2551